Inside Looking Out

To Gay,
Enjoy the read.
Alfred Colo
2008

Alfred Colo

To order additional copies of this book, contact:
Xlibris Corporation
1-888-795-4274
www.Xlibris.com
Orders@Xlibris.com
43672

DEDICATION

To all nature lovers everywhere, who don't have the writing skill to express what they see and hear, just beyond the porch, or from inside the house windows—looking out:

I trust that this endeavor enables me to speak for all the gardeners, bird watchers and animal aficionados, who are sometimes just too busy tending the flowers to smell them, let alone to document their observations for sharing with a wider audience at large.

Alfred Colo

Acknowledgement

I sincerely appreciate the artistry and friendship of the many guides and influences over my eighty years of living, who directly or indirectly have had an impact on my writing style: what I see, hear and feel about what is real, and what may seem so.

The heightened speech of poetry elevates what one has to say, to a place more lovely than what may be commonly perceived. This collected mixture of poetry and prose, adds the spice to what may be seen as ordinary, to what is viewed as extra-ordinary in nature's ever-shifting world on this, our fragile, global-warming, highly-endangered Kingdom of: plants, animals, birds of air and fish in the sea, overseered by us human stewards of all the creation we inhabit.

May God give us the wisdom to protect and preserve the bountiful treasures we have been so abundantly blessed with. Hearing the inconvenient truth isn't always an easy pill to swallow, but must—if we are to continue to survive in cohabitation with our neighbors: wild or domesticated, worldly or special, from this moment in time and well into the future time allotted us. The more prudent we become, the longer this planet will remain healthy and productive, yielding and beautiful as the very first garden, The Eden we inherited!

Gratefully,
Alfred Colo

Introduction

I am ALFRED COLO of New Fairfield, CT; I've been actively writing for seemingly all of my adult life; as a waiter for twelve years (1950-'62), I compiled a journal of observations from the other side of the counter, while composing love songs and writing lyrics, at first with collaborators, then alone, when I became deft enough to do so.

From 1980-1984, as a member in good-standing and as Vice President, I started a monthly newsletter for The Famous Coney Island Polar Bear Club in Brooklyn, NY, until re-settling from my pied-a-tere in N.Y.C.-to a residence in New Fairfield; Fate brought me to rescue and to care for a good friend, stroke victim, for nine years of care-giving until his death in 1993; out of 'UR' and feeling much as Abraham in this strange Promised Land, devoid of inner city conveniences, I learned to cope with the cards I was dealt, and began to drive and developed other country skills I had not been taught to rely upon before.

After a thirty something absence from any sort of religious affiliation, Pastor Rand Peabody came to the rescue with a wheel chair for Hans' sister, Mary, free from the Red Cross. Being a stone's throw away, and a non-driver at first, he invited me to visit; I was able to wheel Hans to their services at The first Reformed Church in CT—on Ball Pond. Rev. Peabody offered help and solace at a much needed time, and had become a mentor for my early bible studies and subsequent attempts at Inspirational Verse, resulting in two volumes of "Chapters 'n' Verse", later to become "The Inspired Word". My prolific output has steadily grown in maturity and volume until the present day.

Caring for an invalid, legally-blinded by a major stroke, I could no longer work at the piano for fear of disturbing Hans, I turned to the more silent means of creative expression, then joined a Creative Writers' Workshop at the church, in whose publications some of my early efforts at writing were included.

Since 1984, I reported and photographed for the local weekly, N.F. Citizen News, which later included four years of annual P.R. writings for the Local Hospice Fund Raising Chapter here, and numerous, diverse poems on wide ranging topics from: love to seasons, weather, nature, holidays, months, etc. As a member of RSVP, I volunteered to write for their news letter, and also to submit wits—and pieces, along with poetry to the NF. Senior Sun Times newsletter.

Further, the NF Library agreed to catalogue 2 Volumes of my Inspirational Poetry, and Advent/Christmas, and Lenten/Easter booklets, written and illustrated for The United Methodist Church and later The Congregational Church I currently attend, as an only octogenarian tenor in a mostly female choir.

I gradually submitted entries of my work: for contests and further publication in fifteen poetry anthologies to:

> The World of Poetry
> The National Library of Poetry
> The International Society of Poets.
> I have been the proud recipient of:
> 20 award of Merit Certificates
> 8 Golden Poet Awards
> Numerous Editor's Choice and
> Semi-finalist certificates.

In 2005 I joined the NF Library Creative Writers' Workshop, and began to present my work to the public in open-mike poetry reads.

In 2007, as part of the NF Senior Center talent show, I was also privileged to read selected poems on Seniority.

My current aim is to continue to grow and to create self-publications, that I may leave a legacy and not die unsung.

Here is an original poem, expressive of: who I am, what I do, and what I hope to become.

I AM A POET

What am I, "You well may ask?"
A poet is what I am,
Who I am, how I feel, what I do.
Sunlight in the shadows
Is where I live and what I celebrate.
How can I teach someone to react,
To become this poetry?
What does the soul need to say
That I may pass down.
On all it means to be poetic?
What is so illusive
That craves to find expression
In an indefinable turn of way?
The poet is the key in the door,
Who unlocks the mysteries
Of some splendid, special swirls
Of sensitivities, serendipities.
Will I ever attain the deepest powers
Of which words are capable?
How shall I live-up-to the words that come
In the wee hours—often late, I create?
For this art to live up to me,
To be great, is more
Than I dare contemplate.
I thank God for entrusting
A portion of His magic
To this humble vessel,
And hope He is pleased with the result.
Yea, I, a poet may be,
But He is the pen!

Alfred Colo

Table of Contents Inside Looking Out

PART 1: WINTER

Snow Prints

Daylight reveals
what dark night conceals:
Snow prints and deer drops
at foraging pit stops.

Nature detects snow-printed tracks,
often expected—soon
after a fast fallen snow.

Crossing, criss-crossing,
the hungry night spent,
spurred on by instinct,
not by accident.

Knocks by their antlers,
I'd oft' heard before,
treks in the open I saw,
trailed up to my door.

Searching for morsels
through garbage they sped,
thankful to tank up
on nocturnal bread.

Resourceful God's creatures,
so deprived, would not thrive,
but for our unfinished courses,
attracting them to arrive,
without a reservation,
for self-preservation.
I never had Lyme's disease,
not even a twist!

Alfred Colo—2004

The Uninvited

Herded deerhooved tracks
braided poke-holed paths
upon December's snow.
No, it isn't hard to trace
the trail of hunger's face,
it follows to avail itself,
guardedly scouring on
long-shadowed lawns,
without being spooked.

One can almost smell
the scent of craving,
starving to the bone,
then burping into audible
groans of satisfaction.

Can we not excuse,
if not condone, their nocturnal,
moon-lit forays: quests as
forbidden guests upon
the tables of the uninvited?
Having invaded their own habitats,
is not turnabout fair play?

Alfred Colo—2004

Just Enough Snow For A Snowman

There's just enough snow for a snowman,
just enough fall for a snowball fight.
Just enough snow for a snowman,
quite enough fluff if you stuff it tight.
(Hee-hee, Ha-ha, Ho-ho!)

There's just enough snow for a snowman,
just enough white on the dirt outside.
Nothing can clean like a snowman.
Just give him a broom and he's charcoal-eyed.
(Hee-hee, Ha-ha, Ho-ho!)

Doff on a hat for the cold,
So's he can rough-it outdoors.
He'll need a pipe he can hold.
Wrap on a scarf and he's yours . . . !

There's just enough snow for a snowman,
Not enough, though, for an avalanche,
But just enough snow that can bend a branch or two,
And just enough snow for a snowman—for you!

Hand him a hat and a muff.
Put on a vest and a glove.
Slip on your specks so he'll see
What you've created to love!

There's just enough snow for a snowman,
Just enough ice for a belly wop.
It'd be nice, had it hadn't stopped so soon.
But, there's just enough snow for a snowman
to cheer us up brighter than noon!

I'm happy. Ho-ho, 'cause there's just enough snow
for a snow man, full as a moon!
('T' sno foolin'!)

Alfred Colo

When The Snow Is Falling

When the snow is falling,
In my mind—
Is where I am
With you;
Far away recalling,
Something right, once,
In my heart,
Ringing true.
When first-love was,
Real and fresh and new,
Innocence was too.
Then the snow was falling,
Just as we were falling,
Young in years of yore,
But alas, no more.
Out the winter's cold
Came a blast:
Standing starkly,
Stiff and old,
Feeling how it felt,
Reeling at what might have been,
Mem'ries melt away now,
As the snow is falling.
Urging me not to
Cling to a luckless past,
Wailing winds,
Born of fallen snow
And love lost,
Nudge me along at last,
To learn to sing
Its lonesome song.

Alfred Colo—2000

New Year 2006

The new year start of 2006 fared no better than 2005's horrendous weather and resultant devastations. Just because a ball drops at midnight in Times Square, NY, to mark a new year, doesn't mean it will be any better, different, or easier; nature just keeps rollin' along at its own pace, no time table for her. That being said, on the first Tuesday after new year's day, while the rest of our nation was besieged with record-rising west coastal tides and mud slides, and with Oklahoma and Texas burning brush wild fires going up in smoke, we here in the north east coastal communities, were pelted by a nasty nor'easter, with snow accumulations of up to one and a half feet in some areas, recalling one of the bitterest storms on record, the likes of which, only 1993 could compare—in my view, in my memory over 20 years in these parts. With only a one day's respite to lick the frost wounds, another storm system gathered momentum, sweeping the area with a wet, icy snow. Pretty as it was, though, my appreciation wore thin as I watched over-laden tree limbs bend and break under the pressure. A neighbor's snow blower barely-skimmed the icy-wet road surfaces, leaving the rest to sand-shovel, melt or surface-drive-over, assuming one luckily had all wheel drive. I did. Calendar schedules flew off the charts, as cancellations and rescheduling mounted daily. Lunches at the local senior center in New Fairfield, were missed, as was Tai Chi class and returns due at the library having to be renewed by phone. Bible study and choir practice, too, were called "on account-a:" even trekking my garbage down a slippery slope, became a dangerous, unwise attempt. When an alert, considerate visiting neighbor saw me near-miss a slip-slide, she asked if she could help me cart to the curb, the rest of my holiday clean up disposables and recyclables. The attic is now lighter and I dare say, less likely to suffer congestive-corrugation, a trusty box cutter made light of and easier to handle.

I fully intended to stretch-display the Christmas decor until the also-red Valentine's day, but one so snow-bound, could only wax stir-crazy if all that wasted time were not put to more productive use. So,—down and away went Christmas up in a day, the New Year Day after.

I did manage to resolve some financial and other pending matters, aimed at a solution to reduce out-of-control credit card spending, with attempts at payback, by switching to lower-offered APR rates. I'm not so sure that: "borrowing from Peter to pay Paul is the solution; only time and finance charges will tell.

Feeling exhausted but better organized, I shoveled out the snow capped terrace, at best, to cut and sand a path from steps to entrance, before another icing made the cake more impossible to cut. I tried to keep ahead with each soggy shovel full on to grass, flower beds and shrubs: so much easier to water in season by hose. Each shovel-toss represented nourishment and insulation, recycled. Beaded traces of animal life, cut visible paths in the snow, a short time ago, thawed from a white Christmas, and just begun to display a full, green grass garden view of terra firma before the pelting began in earnest to coat everything in the sameness of a common denominator. After turning 79 years old at just before Christmas, I thought I'd be better off living south, where snow birds flock; then again, would I prefer a hurricane to a nor'easter? No way! It's a trade-off, each with its own pros and cons. Ya go for as far and as long as you can, where you are, until age or steam run out, whichever comes first.

I readily understand now, why the suicide rate in Nordic European countries is so high. Dismal days can play tricks on a depressed mind, about to explode.

Thursday's a.m. view from my bedroom, on to an early fog, urged me back to the warmth and coz of another hour's roll-over, interrupted by a phone from the dentist, offering a cancellation opening from my hygienist, I could not 'fill' for a hail storm of reasons. If I had wooden teeth, would my mouth be better off, I wondered? History never recorded any complaint from a Washington denture, by George!

As the day wore on, the sun shone brightly and warm on a half-consumed, what-to-do-with day, already whited out. My only salvation was: reading, TV viewing, organizing and compiling a year's-worth of Christian writings for this year's Advent/Easter church booklet. Well ahead of these efforts I began to cheer on a more positive note, the pending implications of a new year, with an ear still far out of touch, with a window view of thoughts to think 'outside the box', flooding my mind. The week-end should clear, enough to get me moving with a zest for as yet unbroken resolves, aiming to be solved with somewhat less than great expectations of a better year to honk my horn about. Celebrate with me, the new arrival of 2006's diapered infant, a second one in two months. Last spring must've started a baby boom of sorts, ya think?

Finally, the pickings off remnant supplies of food, have lowered the larders bare enough to go on another binge-shopping-spree. Won't that make Shaw's Supermart's registers jingle its bells in snow banks all the way to their own bank?

I presume the squirrels' nut supply hasn't run out as yet this winter, since I haven't seen any about. Where do squirrels squirrel any how, I wonder? Have a happy! Peace!

—Alfred Colo

Sole Survivor

A Japanese red maple leaf,
the sole survivor of Fall,
yet clings in crimson,
fragile relief,
still singing
in its barren bird cage
of brittle branches,
now hung with precious pearls
in beaded strands
of frozen rain,
loosely strung
'round its naked neck.

Alfred Colo—2005

Snowed In

When you're snowed in
And under the weather,
Rise above it,
And get over it.

Alfred Colo—1992

Hot Topic: Winter That Wasn't

Where's Winter"?
Not even a flurry!
Buds are sprouting
flowers in a hurry;
Trees are most confused,
but not amused
By record-breaking highs,
before their very eyes.
Denver, in an avalanche of snow,
took the worst of
Winter's cursed woe!

So, what's up with this weather?
Calendars say, January, temperatures read April,
and unseasonably warm. Many parts of America are
balmy as Spring, this so-called Winter.
Warm spells like this are often attributed to
Global Warming, but this year's culprit is El Niño.
That's why, some got and others get—no snow, locking
cold air up in Canada until June breezes blow.

Even viruses, bugging their best in the cold,
are driving the rest of us—nuts, with flu-coughing colds,

I'm told. This strange weather flu season's launch surge,
was late in arriving this year, but it's never too late,
they urge, to get your flu shot, you hadn't got.

Heat and other sales are way off, as costs for clearing snow,
and demands at rock salt stands, are running rather low.

Reservoirs, too, depending on Spring snow melts to
bolster any lack of water supply, are not getting
moisture from our unfriendly skies.

So, get out your shorts and don on your bathing suits
for an unsteady New Year's calendar of warmth and
good cheer in the weeks ahead.

If I spoke too soon, (mea culpa)—if not, well,
jump in anyhow! Perhaps you'll find the Winter that
wasn't here,—there.

The hottest topic this side of the tropics,—is
what's happening in our neck of the woods.

That's your weather!

Alfred Colo—January 2007

Moon Sketch

O'er my Gothic garden fence,
Full 'round, four A.M. high,
Shone a pallid, green-cheese-moon,
Fixed, frozen in the sky.
Light cast shadow branches on—
A 'white board,' back yard lawn,
Like stupendous tentacles
Of octopi with brawn.
Unlike clear reflections
In a near-by limpid pool,
Curved and sprawling contours bent
With randomness, the rule.
Strewn upon uneven drifts,
A strand of light-bright gems,
Sparkled on the snow banks, where—
A buried bush half stems.
From my bedroom window twinkled—
Starshine jewels of night,
Many years beyond the moon,
Through galaxies of flight.
On this morn of calm before
Another 'front' would form,

Forecast for the morrow brews—
A new, unwelcome storm.
Dumped-upon so many times
By blasts already felt,
Would the moon and stars could thaw-
The ice and snow, to melt.
With the winter, but half o'er,
I yearn for early Spring.
Alas, this winter's discontent
Is all it seems to bring.
Tenaciously, and seldom seen
In these here parts before,
The North East could not loose the grip,
Each cold-snap had in store.
Moon light pierced my drap'ries drawn
For undistur-bed rest,
'Woke this poet from a slumber,
As if by request . . . .
Poised was I with pencil, this
Inspired turn occurred:
Earth stretched out its canvas, As
The moon sketched in each word . . . .

Alfred Colo

White Rain

Fell down straight
through a maize this morning,
from a windless sky,
etching the greige
of its dreary blackboard
with chalk-white scratches,
decorating with light deposits
of left-over Christmas,
New Year snow.

Black birds dip and rise
approvingly, in their near-distant,
winter play ground,
stretching their wing tips,
searching for sustenance,
from the freezer
of this day's menu,
while finding a new voice
to caw with,
while White Rain
spreads a table.

Alfred Colo—2005

Winter Workout

Dawn burst in golden sunshine, over a virgin snow, and frigid air, crisp as night, shivering with stars. I greeted this lazy morn by opening the automatic garage door, to air out the basement and ground floor bedroom, then swung open, the window sliders to catch the cool cross current.

Tire tracks lay looking like a printed roadmap of braided, six-lane highways, showing my self-taught maneuvers, necessary for tight-space-entry from a non-turn-'round road: point left, reverse, right ahead and in house.

The warmth of sunny rays and protected extremities, prompted a usual, daily routine of Tai Chi exercise to get the juices flowing through a still lethargic carcass. Beside the indoor fuel tank, lay buckets of salt-sand mix, prepared for spreading iced-over tracks on such a day as this, to allow my SUV easy exit to my destinations of choice. The caked bucket required loosening before using on road and steps, leading to an upper, shoveled deck. The snow-cover no longer glistened, once sanded, but cleared a safe way down a slippery slope towards the mail box, holding yesterday's neglected pick up.

An unfamiliar bird sound, dot-dashed its lonely messages in alternating staccato triplets, followed by double beeps.

From a near distance, a cawing choir of crows, chanted a morning anthem, until breakfast feeding silenced their performance.

My back-saving, curved handle snow shovel, working out the rest of my body kinks, paved my way back to a hardy meal of my own, with a solo in my heart singing: "All's well in my corner of the world, insulated from current horrors of a less-peaceful universe, ravaged by wars in another clime of bloodier desert sands, working out its own usefulness, the reverse of melting down.

Alfred Colo—January 2005

Yucca

Along the property lines,
Yucca plant spikes
pierce the snows of bleakness
with green swords,
finding their grey winter marks;
the green of yuccas
is the single solace
the eye can scan
on a silent canvas of starkness.
While patiently waiting
for Spring's torch
to rekindle the darkness
with new bursts of bloom,
they re-load their guns
with new shoots in their holsters,
to bolster the great outdoors,
once freed of the bite
of winter's jaws,
and the frozen grip of its claws.
Fresh spikes of white clusters, then,
will fix bayonets at point,
to do battle along side
the swords of comrades,
until they themselves
become the fallen heroes.

Alfred Colo—2005

Fog

Dropped on nimble feet,
remnants of cloud,
shrouding mobility
like Halloween ghosts,
sheets of night,
invading clear sight,
blinding the road
with puffs of :
cotton-candy-like
fleeces of wool.
Fog spells danger,
swarming as soup
at the lick-of-it.
Sorry for deer,
frozen in fear,
before as you veer,
out from each tick-of-it,
stunned by the headlights of night.
Fog crippled my way,
inching each slice like a knife,
while hugging for life
to the yellow center divide,
desperately trying to avoid a road kill,
all too easy to hit head on.
Through glassy-eyed targets
I groped in fear, and hoped
they'd soon disappear
from this treacherous road,
I drove home on alone
in a dense and intensely
frightening January fog.

Alfred Colo—2005

False Spring

Mid-February's chilly evening sunset, took my breath and eyes by pleasant surprise: Through leafless tree sticks, shone a rainbow-colored sky, layered in magnificent strands: starting on a blue horizon, upwards in successive strata of aqua and rosy hues, topped by pale pinks, fusing white clouds, alternating a mix of greys and powder blues; the vision hadn't lasted long, but clicked in my mind's eye for transference to a poetry-palletted paean of words, not intended to compete, but supplement actual water-color strokes on another canvas.

By this time, snow had melted through the lawn's greening grass, too short for cutting, though emerging as a kind of false Spring. Unstored-for-winter garden trappings began to mirror the sky: the blue, upturned water barrel cistern, a forest green, moulded, unfolding garden cart, leaned against a supportive shed, and a tattered taupe, bluish mulch pile cover, aiming to reduce Fall's crisp fullness of leaves.

I then gathered an arm-full of fallen, snapped tree limbs, to lighten upcoming, pre-mowing preps, soon to arrive. The air whipped clean, as a still saturated lawn sank beneath my feet. A recently read garden article, planted a seed in my mind, to pick a tall vase-full of budding forsythia branches, for indoor early forcing in warm water, changed daily; their cheery yellow blossoms were soon to complement, hardy, seasonal purple pansies.

After the harsh days, a feathered clique of robins, when not battling inclement weather, huddled together on the bark sides of back yard fruit trees, pecking for food from its feeding branches, while dusty miller plants, struggled to make a second year comeback.

Yet dormant, the rest of the garden won't take much longer to arise from slumber, into full-blown contributors to spring at last. Yucca plant spikes, drooping from frost, strived to make an unsteady stand. Have we the same confidence to handle winter changes, or do we often allow them to slip away unnoticed like now visible, half-fallen diagonal tree-trunk victims, clung in the arms of grieving standbys?

A pale, rosy gossamer haze, hovered at the tree tops, joining a mountain sky over Ball Pond north, offered sublimer vestiges of rare February sunsets, traditionally coldest, this time of year, but still breathing, unseasonally warm temperatures.

A stretch of Tai Chi warm-ups, limbered by nature's generosity, uplifted my body and soul, at my old, New Fairfield pied-a-tere sanctuary, sending false messages of tentative emergings.

All's well, at least for the moment, in my little world, high on the wine of bottled poetry; tomorrow then, may have other unique surprises up the sleeve of winter's lock, which I anticipate with wide-eyed wonder, or not, unless gathering storm warnings conspire to make a liar out of Pauxitony Phil!

Alfred Colo—February 2005

A Dusting Of Snow

One dusting of snow and the ashen grounds paled before a gray pond, while trees took on the look of powdered sugar on a bundt cake. There was a frosty edge to this late January dawn, and a sheet draped the ledge of a mystical morn. In the East, a rising sun promptly poured light into the dip of a near distant hill. Through an open window I wafted several whiffs of brisk morning pick-me-up.

In another six or so weeks, ground-hog-predictions notwithstanding, this scene can change from gray to life, and Spring will sip its first brew of ol' man winter's melt-down. Early croci will peek over the new year's white down comforter, and forsythia will comb its long hair in graceful arcs of golden glory.

A.M.'s alarm clock punctuated my reverie with reveille, as I imagined American boys, our brave recruits in 1996 Bosnia, in first assembly of the day. Randomly spaced purveyors of death, buried underground; land mines coiled to explode from multiple traps with destruction in their springs.

While winter pays its annual debt to Spring for the price-of-life from scattered seed in autumn's furrows, the sands of time are sifting through a fractured hour glass. Far from the fray and the nightmares of possible conflict time for the moment at least, stands still. A dusting of snow spreads tranquilly over more peaceful beds, tucked in—safely at home—here in New Fairfield.

Alfred Colo

Even In February . . .

(Weather or Not)

Leaves and grasses have been so long covered that I've almost forgotten what they look like. Determined to find some evidence of life beyond my own confinement, I forced my lethargic slump to stretch, to see what was not evident through my window: Small berries and emerging bits of color clung to icy, stark stems, stripped of leaves, stubbornly refusing to be smothered by snow, rekindled my own desire and hope that spring would not be too far off, give or take current predictions of a ground hog's shadow.

Heavy seasonal snow-on-snows, once bright comforters over shivering grounds, ice over before turning slushy and gray as Monday's dirty laundry. Bare branches groping sky ward, beg the sun to show some shine from behind oppressive cloud blocks. I too, am color-starved and hunger for light. Mid February, traditionally the coldest time of year, seems lifeless. But today, resisting all forces and viruses that have sheltered me indoors too long since the start of 2003, I bundled myself in protective layers to brave the freezing digits that nip the nose and hands and toes.

Have you too, been disturbed, downcast and restless lately? You're not alone. Has your heart and flesh felt lifeless and frigid, as if in February failure? Take heart, then, your funny valentine will warm you. Celebrate!

Recalling the blizzard of ninety six, even in February, when I felt too blue to notice the doldrums and chill, still, we thankfully had each other and most of the really needed essentials, in the bitterest 'winter of discontent' in recent memory.

Tiny pockets of color helped me rediscover my intimate love affair with nature, while joyfully reassuring me that, whatever the weather of my feelings', new life lies astir under a seemingly dormant state of hibernation: never too far away, ever active, optimistically poised and alert, EVEN IN FEBRUARY, on the brink of Spring, on the edge of renewal . . . Just the right warmer weather ER must cure my ennui, or incline me South for an instant RX . . . I'm ready!

"No storm can ever stop Spring from coming", it is said. Birds will return after the chill and snow vanish, sometime. After toughing-out a pretty rough winter, and with February's last blast behind us, hopefully March and April will be kind and hold no more surprises. But hey, in an El Nino year, anything's possible, right? So . . . , keep your fingers crossed till we're completely over the hill and sliding down March into the woods of Spring once again. I will not be sorry anytime soon, to see this winter gone at last! Any arguments? I didn't think so.

Alfred Colo—2003

The Look Of Winter

Jack Frost, delivered an icing on 1990's birthday cake. Late Jan.'s and early Feb.'s snows delivered these picture-perfect postcards to New Fairfield. Time stood still for winter's camera to click its shudder as all negatives awaited positive developments:

Warm white wood smoke spiraled through falling snow, vainly attempting to melt its heart.
Gutters, limbs and lines, looked like frozen linguini.
'Snainy' frosted branches transformed treescapes into a fragile crystal wonderland.
Poking picket fences stood silent as sentinels
over their winter white watch.
Snow does not discriminate; its democracy covers all.
No fences can keep it from landing on party lines.
Turgid roads of salted sand, wound serpentine curves through
slushy country sides as reluctant civilization carefully coped through nature's detergent, while trees huddled in frozen silhouettes against Monday's winter white wash.
Unperturbed springs lay dormant under Ball Pond's solid sheets,
as marine life became the 'catch-of-the-day' for avid ice fishers.
Sky and land were a pair of look-a-likes, divided by an uncertain horizon.

Painted houses and evergreens looked like licked stamps
      on white envelopes, ready for delivery.
Layed-back poison ivy must be itching to get under
      our skins.
      Scratch the lot, I say! All in favor say, "Ouch!"
Brazen black birds clawed for morsels and crows cawed
      for crumbs from winter's table.
Feeders serve as silent soup kitchens for the 'seedy-
needy' backyard birds of air.
Squirrels and birds took turns on high wires, admitting
      us to their aerial acts, free of 'charge.' AT&T is
      keeping tabs on their 'Sprints.'
All-at-sea, a listless weather vane's ship launched for
      direction through the storm. Once the giver, now the
      getter, sits on its pointless N.S.E.W. quiver.
Sculptured white plastic bucket arm chairs fringed in
      frozen tassels, sit out in winter upholstery,
      anticipating warmer pullups to spring and
      summer tables.
Invisible roses stick out on thorn bushes of imagination.
Sliding ponds ponder, while kiddy swings yonder, are
      fonder of joyful tots squeaking their hinges.
Semi-severed from mother trees, broken limbs,
      unsteadily clung, are inevitably bent towards
      winter's wood pile.

Alfred Colo

Oh, Winter Sun

An early snow plow clanked to clear a sanded path,
And under the watchful blue of mother sky's melting eye,
Dead trees, felled for firewood,
Lay log-split, where stumps now stood.
Chimneys spewed forth cozy curls of spiral ash,
While fresh-ground coffee perked the kitchen air,
And I lay snuggled there—warm as toast.
Night kicked off its slippers,
When a smiling ray cracked through my shaded window,
Whereupon this word picture penned itself
At the easel of day.
In the full array of 'A-sol-e'!
      OH, WINTER SUN,
Poised on the haunches of dawn,
Readied to burst
As the hush of morn sprang to purr . . .
Cozily tucked under its sleepy white quilt,
Nature yawned, as bird-calls sounded reveille:
Awake turbulent world, from your icy grip;
Purse your cold-snapped, white-capped, limpid lip;
Shake your snow-laden sinews of their shroud;
Stretch your frosted fingers to a cloud—
Up—out, to and fro . . .
Ho Ho! . . . . Hello!
Welcome in, OH WINTER SUN!
Warm this icicled breast.
Find my faint-pulsed heart.
Was it still beating, I wondered,
As I lay fumbling for it?
What was slumber's toll
For a restless roll in Morpheus' arms?
Jack Frost's deep-freeze—ended.

Alfred Colo

Jack Frost

JACK FROST,
Why have you withered the flowers?
Must you cruelly and fiercely
Strip the forests,
Bare of shivering,
Of color and sound,
And scare the tweets
Out of birds,
Sweet on the honey
From bees?
Swiftly I'd follow
The path of the swallow,
Far from the range
Of your fury and roar,
To wave you farewell
And welcome no more,
From some sunnier,
Balmier,
Friendlier,
Frostless shore, JACK!

Alfred Colo

Ice Break

February's weather is now history. My first clocking of this year's thaw on Ball Pond: Wednesday the 26th, about 12:30 p.m. The uneasy groans beneath the frozen surface, created restless rumblings, sounding like muffled distant thunder. Cracks formed where sounds were heard. Then . . . the ice broke!

An avid woodpecker, unperturbed by the happening, punctuated a momentary lull. In its gray coat, its pointed beak pecked away. As this sap-searching, hard-hatted red head, braced for another 'round,' it instantly became part of the woodwork as I neared, resuming its mind-boggling tap-tap-taps when I passed.

A watch dog's lonely staccato barks announced an approaching stranger like a blare of trumpets. On guard at its thankless stand, a long rope and a chill air were its only reward.

Trucks and autos rolled past at lazy intervals, grinding . . . purring. Along the ice's edge below Route 39's north pond end, unfrosted crystal cameos revealed frozen clusters of fallen leaves and twigs, preserved at 'onslaught time.' Other reminders of Autumn rust, rustled above in sharp wintry gusts. Tree branches whisped the sky in crackling aerobics, poking their brooms through power pole parallels along the sand-strewn route.

The pond's ice-marred surface lay frost-bitten, glistening in a glaze of 'figure eights,' and an undulating maze of ski marks and snowmobile overlapping patterns of tire tracks. Still trapped, the charred remains of 'once-merry' Christmas trees, out-lived their cheer and long since, their warmth. So, too, lay clumps of burned logs left by warming ice lubbers as their bon fires crackled and snapped.

On February 28, in brilliant (a.m.) sunshine, my brisk walk around the pond was conspicuous by the absence of other human stirring. Nature, never at the office, provided 'in-residence' responses in fuller measure; a babbling brook, cawing crows, melting snow, myriad bird migration rest stops. Weekly trash out for pickup, lay by delivered news, ready to be read. Varied mailboxes stood at attention, some half-open, to receive delivery.

A quickened gait primed my dormant hulk. My cheerful heart pumped renewed vigor through its listless life lines. Spring sprung! Ice broke, my winter blues with 'haute-couture-anticipation' for a whole new wardrobe of fresh greens, yellow, whites and pinks, forthcoming from nature's tailor.

March, the next unpredictable, contender to February's throne, would enter lamb-like on the first, tenderly alive—but how harsh would its lion-hearted roaring sound at month's-end exit?

So much for HIBERNATION! Let's take an ICE BREAK . . . Popsicles anyone?

Alfred Colo

Snow Day

(Presidents' Day)

Winter draped a predicted over-night nine or so inch dressing of still dropping, non-stopping snow, onto morning's chilly, pristine silence. Howling winds, growling through open spaces, joined the clankings of plough trucks, returning for sand to make roads safer and more passable.

This Presidents' Day, my 1976 National Flag, furled stiffly in the wind, which wound it 'round the diagonal pole, off my balcony, now trimmed white with wooly-puffed decorations of warm insulation. Summer screens, attached year-'round, semi-obscured my view with oblique snowflake trappings, as if through a sieve.

After the previous thaw, a new mid-west snow track blasted the North East with belated Valentine shivers, across tracks of blurred property lines. Soon the holiday dig-outs would follow, without any last minute presidential pardon to reprieve my reluctant shoulders. My first priority was to remove the snow-covered cement-cracked balcony, built over a ceiling-stained bedroom below; this effort helped deter seepage from further melt downs, causing more extensive damage. Then, I cleared a path through the terrace and further stripped by hand and shovel, the snow-blown road, leading home: Surely, I thought later, this must have been the cause of pains from last year's rotator cuff tear operation. Ouch!

Alberta spruces, planted triangularly, donned fetching snow cone caps, stood sentinel at the gates, offering little or no relief to weather invasions, and far from drifting desert sands of Iraqi unrest.

Feeling secure and cozy-warm inside, the winding-down storm quickly divested itself of an avalanche of airlifts. I thought to compose love poetry, as did Dr. Zhivago, in his unwinterized summer cottage retreat, holding an icicle pen-pour of sentient ink: the rhymes and dreams of happier, less fractured times. Soon the sound and smell of fresh-ground, perking coffee, lured my lips toward its cup for an a.m. pick-me-up sip. There I lazily programed the day, already marked by a flight of a cawing crows against a pregnant sky, spewing spirals of wood-burning smoke. Good time, I thought, to finish reading a half-read book with 'novel' twists, rather than tuning in to bad news reports with sad endings, peppered with commercial intrusions, hawking presidential sales pitches. This snow day seemed not an opportune time to search for bargains. Rather, snow days like this one are selfishly all mine, to do with as I pleased. This day was begging to be seized, and so I did by first gripping the wide, open handle of the coffee mug, bearing the reminder: "Carpe Diem"! Mañana would be another day, but not until the final surprise of this one: That snow day night, riding to a Wednesday Lenten soup and bible study, an enormous, low-hung full moon appeared through my Subaru windshield, dead ahead. "No, it couldn't be a Harvest Moon," I pondered, "not this time of year," so I I dismissed the Presidential sighting with a Jonny Mercer lyric of: "It's only a Paper Moon," tune, singing in my head, along the winding road.

Alfred Colo

Lions In, Lambs Out

Nowadays an awful lot of roaring
And selfish yelling goes on:
Our entertainment and work places, are noisy.
T.V. is like a hungry den of felines
On a selling attack, in which
Few survive the night of broken continuity,
Without being devoured by
Boring, too-loud commercials.
Seldom do we hear a silent persuader,
Selling its product benefits
By capturing, not demanding attention.
Haven't we been deluged enough
Into turned-up, forced acceptance?
When was the last standout point
That really caught your interest
With the shocking waves of nothing—
But the refreshing sound of silence?
How nice was that, not to have to
Channel-surf, nor silence that segment
for a brief moment of serenity,
Before the program resumes and
Another commercial grabs you?
March's mantra of the month ought be:
'Be wise as serpents, not loud as lions,'
Recalling that great thinkers
Sought and found solutions
In simple silence and relative peace.

March seems a proper month
To practice lowering the disturbing decibles
In the blatant voices of our strident lives,
This Lent of sacrificial "give-ups".
See how it pushes like a lion,
Leaving us gently, as a lamb.
More often, we need to step out
From the roaring crowd, for a lion's share
Of the solitude of silence,
Without needing to excuse,
Turning a few loud things down
To a whispering halt.
Enough already!
How high a price must a viewer pay,
To endure such privacy invasion?
How dumb, to numb defenseless,
Captured audiences into channel submission?
It's a problem, for sure,
In search of a cure!
Ah well, Spring is coming;
We won't be so locked indoors,
Looking to a box for diversion.
Let's step out the box into nature's backyard,
To hear nicer noises of welcome intrusions.

Alfred Colo
March 2004

Another Drop Takes New Fairfield By Storm

Just when we all thought after the last blizzard, that mother nature would give us a break, another winter blast belted the area. And when February turned the corner, March came roaring in like a lion!

On Thursday afternoon I heard a hugh thunder crack that shook me to the rafters. My first thought was: This is the 'Big One', given the seriousness of an international standoff and the impending war with Iraq, plus terrorist activity threats. I immediately rushed to the TV to see if there were any reports of another attack here; alas, the only onslaught was the continuous falling snow. To stay ahead of the rapid accumulation, I shoveled a path to my letter box to learn what else was news and to clear a path in front of the box for the mail carrier.

I'm weary of 'Snow White' covering us since last year's white Thanksgiving until this, the latest, and hopefully final 'blow'.

Business must be booming for ski resorts and costly snow removals. The best advice for black ice: Take it slow; treacherous travel icing conditions made tri-state-area commutes no piece of cake in this winter's scenario of flurry flakes, potholes and ice patches. Our state got the heaviest snow accumulations on a bleak day of fender benders and spin outs, as temperatures dropped on this latest snow-down. As if to copy-cat the mess, the stock market also took a dive.

I'd welcome more than a tired weather advisory to lift my spirits and to point me in the opposite direction from snow. Move over winter. Give Spring a chance. It ain't been easy for anyone, especially senior citizens. Enough is enough already. Alas, we all complain about the weather, but are helpless to do a thing about it, except to snow blow it, or shovel it and pile it up under protest. Can St. Patrick's Day, do you suppose, be the charm that makes the greening of Spring more welcome than ever? Don't get your hopes up too high just yet, however, when experience and history teach us to expect snow even in April. I'm not grinning, but will just have to bear it, like the rest of us.

On an optimistic note: 10 free flowering trees, coming from the National Arbor Day Foundation, should make a world of difference to my landscape, and not to mention, my disposition, as well as the stretch on my pocket and aching back. This record-breaking winter of snow-on-snow-on-snow, is making me awfully tired of white; I think we're all ready for another change of decor—to take us by storm: Rain would be nice! You choose.

CAVEAT: Please, don't pray for a white Easter; you may just
get one!

Alfred Colo

Nor'Easter

After a nor' easter hit New Fairfield, pelting gusty drifts of nine-or-so inches of steady seasonal snow, a bright-shining sun burst through a clear-blue, cloudless sky, warming the area, with not even a hint of wind. Though still chilly, even through my, thirty-something-year-old brown wool and tasseled robe, it felt like a spring harbinger, charging me with an energy, unmatched all winter, to get things going like: carting down the garbage for pickup at the curb. Following my own car tire tracks down the hill, ruts, grooved in unblown snow, about an inch from the ground surface, glistened glassily under a noon-day sun, hastening the defrosting process. Luckily my brand new AWD Subaru Impreza Sport Wagon, easily skipped over what used to be: slippery, tire-spinning, vain attempts at getting off the ground; with disparate tire pressures at thirty two front, and twenty nine rear, propulsion had just the right kick to climb the hill, my Nissan Max often breached for lack of power to go the distance.

I prefer to cart garbage down on the same day of pickup, to avoid spills from scavengers, pushing over the can to pick over the source of smell's attraction. Often, after a nocturnal meal, whatever animal spread the table, not even a small attempt at clean-up was noticed. Their: "I hate to eat and run attitude" is definitely unacceptable on my watch! Across the road, Ball Pond was still frozen over, as a few colorful skaters glided about in figure-eights, attempting to match Winter Olympic standards. As I wound my way back up to the house, yet festooned with Christmas, trees, white-laced with snow, formed a pretty post card picture. Dripping icicles fringed the north side of the roof's edges, and hung at both ends in three-feet-long formations from pitched gutters, filling their spill of summer waterings at the prevailing outside room temperatures. Apart from my own foot and tire tracks, deer prints led to the house entrance, where a convenient rotating mulcher stood, saving me longer treks to a more distant, often snowed-in pile.

Through this frigid framework of frost, the lens in my mind's eye, visualized the first flowers of spring life: fragile crocci to daffodils, contrasted with early, hardy pansies in purple dresses, donned for Easter, arriving at the early book ends of March. With Valentine just over, St. Patrick's Day will arrive in Kelly-greens and the smell of corned beef dinner, Celtic celebrations, digested with swallows of beer brews, and Irish coffee. It occurred to me that most winter holidays fall around the colder months, as if someone had planned such activities for none of us to get bored, until warmer weather prompts our own, ambitious spring clean ups, preparing for another summer of fun from the great out of doors, looking in. After the incessant barrages of snow we've had this year, milder weather can't come soon enough for me!

Looking out your window at a pretty shadow of a backyard tree, tracing itself, makes the beauty felt, worth the while getting over winter's doldrums!

Alfred Colo
March 2005

Morning Revelations

I set up my easel to word-paint this morning-after Ground Hog day's revelations: A triangular roof shadow cast the rear image of my home onto slowly-melting snow, uncovering all that winter had hidden from sight: criss-crossing traces of hungry nocturnal foragers, yet revealing proof of passage, soon I shall no longer be able to perceive what game, came and went.

A faint yellow aura hovered on bordering forsythia bushes, offering hope indeed, that Spring might arrive earlier than predicted: six more winter weeks.

Well basins, submerged around root bases, began to reveal grass and other ever-green touches of welcome. Stones from last Fall's enlarged rear garden patch, skeletal border, again bared the bones in the curvatures of its spine.

Three bowling ball acquisitions from tag sales, reappear on their finial moorings, multi colors, anxious for tournament action down the alley of Spring.

Half of the white, anchored portion of an inaccessible, snowed-in flag pole, stood proudly white against the snow, prepared to prop the remainder of its stored sections to telescope Old Glory whenever weather permits unfurling.

The vegetable garden picket fence, cloned an exact image upon the ground, off the sun's direction, as a round wire fenced-in mulch pile, set brewing used coffee grounds and other kitchen biodegradables in its pot, and ice caps slowly perk onto the melt of a lifeless mix of home recipes for new plant blooms.

In a distance, on the edges, I detected a fallen tree trunk, suspended by surrounding perpendiculars, which had survived winter; I secretly mourned this fallen hero, that couldn't make it back to live another Spring.

On the surface of today's canvas, I could see little signs of life, but know in my heart, it's dormant under-layers will spring ahead in due time for daylight savings. Oops, sorry, I spoke too soon: there goes a snow bird, skipping along the ground. There's a black crow, wide-winging its feathers across the day's canvas sky, towards a huddle of cows, fresh up to its ears in snow, emerging from Blizzard '05, prepared to give milk, white as snow.

A vestige from another day and time, poked its brown slender frame, pretending to pump water after it's disconnection, when lightening struck twice and it had to be put down, still standing beside its cap, mourning any further usefulness, save showing multi-colored layers of peeling paints of yesteryear, now simply a nostalgic garden decoration, handling nothing but its own serpentine curvature, pumping anything but water.

Alfred Colo

"There's No Business Like Snow Business"

(The blizzard of '93—storm of the century)

There's no business like snow business,
Like no business I know.
Everything about it is congealing,
Everything the traffic won't allow.
Nowhere could you get a rush so reeling,
Than when you're wheeling behind a plow.
There's no people like snow people.
They 'Ho' with such gusto!
Even when a nor'easter's about to hit,
And get up to our hips in it,
Still we wouldn't change it
'Cause we got true grit.
Let's git on with the snow.
There's no business like snow business,
When all business is slow.
We got word before the storm had started—
To prepare for damages by dawn;
Listened-up as news breaks were imparted.

We weren't outsmarted, but carried on.
There's no people like snow people,
Who thrive in sub-zero.
Yesterday they told us it could be bizarre,
The night it bowled us over mighty far;
Next day mother nature swallowed up the car.
No way! Where could it go?
There's no business like snow business,
When hail and four winds blow.
Shov'ling out from under wasn't thrilling,
Nor the blinding wind chill blizzard bites.
Helplessly we watched the driveways filling,
And felt unwilling to clear the heights.
There's no people like snow people;
We're cool when we're aglow.
Snow flakes fell from everywhere with lots o'pack.
And when Jack countered with his attack,
We built snow man pow'r that stopped him in his track,
And got on with the show.
There's no business like snow . . . business, that is!

Alfred Colo
March 2003

But Not In March

Snow is a beautiful gift, but NOT IN MARCH! It should fall on Christmas Eve. Snow's decorative benefits can be appreciated in varying degrees through January and half of February . . . BUT NOT IN MARCH!

Others who've had quite enough snow, no longer care to experience new storms.

Snow can be a thing of magic and wonder, and often is, BUT NOT IN MARCH! All we can do is live with the unexpected snows that come in March, but ought not to be dealing with them into Spring. It no longer feels right—or even fair, when sports in southern climes are active with spring training games. There's something out of whack when we must worry about outed power and snapped tree limbs, when infant pokings, through garden soil of incipient buds of promise—are glimpsed.

Birds are expected to arrive by now as well, but are heading back from whence they came, not to contend with late major storms. Storms like this should not be occurring to man or beast, least of all in March . . . Finding cardinals in the snows of January and February, can brighten winter, but not now . . . in March.

The picturesque is more seasonal to capture in photos, BUT NOT IN MARCH!

I can appreciate snow, and relish walking in a fresh fall, unmarred by foot prints. Also, there is a delight in exploring a forest in new snow; I can lose myself tracing wild animal trails, known by their tracks. I'm so nuts about snow, even squirrels envy me; I don't even mind shoveling out the car drive or patio steps to the front door . . . or garage. Just being out here is invigorating and the greatest gift, at any other time, but, ... not when March leaves like a Lion!

Please, no, NOT IN MARCH! Enough's enough!

Alfred Colo—2007

I Remember The Wind

I remember the wind,
the height of the storms,
the fright at the swarms
of the forces I felt,
the fear of how fury deforms.
I remember the wind,
the smell of its death,
the tunnels from hell
which funneled a stench,
welled-up on its breath.
Who knows why these tragedies happen?
The 'ill twists' of fate
can catch some too soon—
off guard, while others too late.
I remember the sounds
of the claps and the shatter,
which whipped without warning,
too fast that dark morning to matter.
Zigzagging scars of destruction and hurt,
sought victims in cars,
caught dwellings of worth,
uprooted hugh trees,
hurled horses and cows off the earth.
Lingering longer in the wake of its dust,
than I care to, I trust, to forget,
was the rip in that wind,
mid-March of the year
I'll remember with taunts of regret.

Alfred Colo—1997

Blizzard 2005

Lifted on white, falling, diagonal confetti, slanting in the wind, a slow, but steady snow accumulation arrived as a first major blast of the year; snow on an old TV set could only pale by comparison to nature's reality channel.

Roads and walks, fast-filled before pushing shovels could barely keep up with the back and fills repeated layerings. Keeping watch of this pelting blizzard, pressed me to imagine what the over-night accumulation could cover and the depths or heights to which this snow would grow.

A twin white birch outside the kitchen window, bore scars of an over-stretched bracing tether, long since snapped, are now being bandaged on the wind side of its crusty bark, with white gauze, to which the driven snow wrapped itself.

Mid noon's over cast, bleek, grey sky, will soon descend on evening shadows, ending the first visible act in silent wonder, as the second act brews all the conflict necessary to resolve dawn's concluding and final act.

Recent world-wide weather patterns have surprised many with untold, unforewarned earth quakes, volcanic eruptions, mud slides, floods, hurricanes and a south Indian ocean tsunami of biblical proportions. One can only speculate if and when the 'Second Coming' is going to fulfill these world-ending signs. What, I wonder, will an upside down sky-tsunami, deluge us with? Perish the thought! If this storm were water-walled, instead of flecking flakefalls, the devastation might be catastrophic.

My impatience at the outcome of this blinding blizzard, must surely cause me to have a restless night. But, come dawn, will I be able to clear the way in time for Sunday's am church service choir sing, or will the Lord's day be unrejoiced and sad in it? It's God's call, and only for us victims of the punch, to figure out what clearance would entail.

Alas, there's not much mortal man can do when weather assails, but talk together about it, until this too shall pass and skies will swell with shine again on every shore. We've become terribly conscious of what the weather is doing as it directly affects us. The snow . . . the rain . . . all these things we live with daily. We're also very conscious of the passing of time as the sun arcs across the sky. Blizzards come and go, not I; I'm willing to stay-put until more sure of foot. I'll survive Blizzard '05, just by stayin' alive until the 'all clear.'

Spring may be just around the corner, but something's blocking the view!

Alfred Colo

Winter's Ballet

Winter snow,
Gently, silently falling,
Drifting, merrily calling,
Beseeches the wind, imploring
Don't disrupt this
Pointing, this prancing,
Our swirling and twirling,
Dipping and dancing,
Retreating, advancing.
Allow winter's ballet
To continue, unintruded.
Dare not compete with
The measured marks
Of its delicate cadence.
Follow its steps;
Mar not their flow.
What musical, mystical.
Magical show!

Pas De Deux

Hope lies heavy
On the doorstep of care,
Following footprints,
Formed in—
The snow trails of frost.
Gripped in the ice-lock
Of winter's jaw,
Can spring be far behind,
Its thaw, too far off?

Alfred Colo—2001

Table of Contents Inside Looking Out

PART 2: SPRING

(A Lament To Spring)

WHERE'S THAT BIRD?

WHERE'S THAT BIRD?
Was it too cold to sing?
Had it heard
that it's too soon for Spring?
Where did it fly?
I wonder why
it had to go,-
leaving me here
another year,
never to know . . . .
WHERE'S THAT BIRD?
Had it gone South or West?
Not a word
out of the Robin's breast.
Surely I miss
hearing its song
cheering me on.
Where are you?
Wonder where that bird is.
Wonder where that lovin' bird has gone!

WHERE'S THAT BIRD?
Can it be skyward bound?
Was it bent,
stirred to seek higher ground?
Feelin' alone,
I may have grown
fonder of you.
Why should I care
If you're not there?
Oh, but I do!
Where's that bird?
Where is that whipporwill?
No wings whirred;
even the air is still.
Oh, how I miss
your melody
sweet as can be?
Where are you?
Wonder where that bird is
Wonder why it left the tree to me!

Alfred Colo—1980

A Silent Wait For Spring

In the marsh—
Life awaits Spring's greening.
To watch its wonder,
Stand there this winter
In the final, pristine hush of the year.
Before life re-awakens
From under the thickest ice,
And from below the deepest snow,
The marsh of silence,
In a matter of weeks,
Becomes a bed of clamor,
Return to marvel again
At its bursts of vitality,
In the blush of, the rush . . . of spring.
What long lay locked
In frozen embrace,
May well survive—
To greet the arrival
Of Spring's revival,
With solar kisses, tenderly placed—
Upon its fragile face . . . .

Alfred Colo—1998

Spring, At Last

Spring is late. Winter's chill
Was still upon it when it came.
While you wait, April will bestow a bonnet on it.
What a dame! Here she comes!

Spring, at last.
I can taste May wine.
I'll be first in line . . . at last.

Spring, at last.
Not too soon to start
Love affairs of heart . . . at last.

Every bird due in,
That flew in, I heard:
Makes the awakening sweet!

Every tree stirrin'
Its buds that were in slumber,
Are out in great number to greet.

Spring, at last.
Visible signs, all around us,
Shaking their hinds to as-tound us.
Spring is here . . . at last.

Spring, at last.
Feelin' fit and fine
Up and down my spine
With love nearly mine . . . at last.

Spring, at last,
Hums a nature tune,
Fills up your ballon . . . then blast!

All the bees and rabbits,
Are at ease in habits,
Making honey and hare.

Every lark and squirrel
In the park were not ill,
But anxious to pair . . . to share:

Spring, at last:
Color means to restore us:
The 'mese-en-scene' is before us . . . not past.
All about us.
No doubt us . . . . aghast.
Spring, I fear, is here
At long, long last!

Alfred Colo
1979/2005

Spring . . . At Last

Wake up, all you couch potatoes. Get off yer butts and out of your ruts, rub winter's sand from your tired eyes and shake off winter's frost. Haven't you heard, it's springtime for early bloomers? Days are getting longer, buds are budding in pastel splashes and the red, red robins are bob-bob-bobbin' along. Warmer weather is perfect for outdoor enthusiasts in pursuit of physical fitness, a jog along an undefined path, a bike ride on a back road, or some early digs in the spring garden. Don't be left out in the cold; warm up to the fact that a new season is definitely here with early predictions for spring . . . So, let's up, up, up and away on a breezy, kite-flyin', wonderful day. Fish are jumpin' and soon it'll be time to check your rod and reel, bait your hooks and try your luck. Oh, what a feeling to reel in a big one!

The buzz is that needles will fly at local quilting bees. If that's your cup-a-tea, try your hand until you're knee-deep in stitches. As for me, I'll join the geese and ducks, the swans and seagulls for a Spring break on Ball Pond.

Sure Signs of Spring

When buzzards are back to Hinkley, Ohio and swallows return to Capistrano . . . when first rains fill reservoirs, excepting the torrential California kind these days of fog and smog, sludge and floods. I'll settle for a nice spring shower or two that knows its limits, is good for gardens while making me feel fresh as a country lane afterwards. Spring is a time when a young man's fancy gets fancier and turns to thoughts of LUV! Love of all sorts is in the Springtime air as spring flings begin the mating season. As the warmer air improves their chances for survival, chirps, caws and honks on the wing return to our area once again singing their songs. Presidential candidates, too, are off to a flying start, hawking their changes, while tossing their hats into the ring of chance in the election process. Incumbents are always hard to beat—but only time will tell if Hillary Clinton is beatable, or on March 20 the official Spring date, will see new shifts in major currents, but will the weather cooperate? No way! Though it may be spring-like in some areas, history proves that others may likely be shoveling up to X number of inches of the 'white stuff,' or drying out from driving, soaking rains. Spring lamb will soon be seen on supermarket shelves, though we may get the lion's share, if March exits like a lamb. This 'baseball replacement thing' is ushering in a new season of spring training . . . Is the end of a strike in sight? "O-oh say, can we see?" Let's hope for a home run—not a strike out!

Calendar:

Spring follows on the heels of the Ides of March on the fifteenth, to the marching bands of Saint Patrick's Day parades; all that wearin' of the green must be a harbinger of sorts. Looking ahead comes April's Fool on day one. On day 2 of April is daylight saving: time to spring ahead one hour. Let's synchronize our watches . . . all together now!

Mid-April is, you guessed it, IRS tax deadline . . . Oh, joy! Well, ya gotta give to Caesar what belongs to Caesar, right? Bad as it sounds we all must pay the freight and share the load. The day after D Day is Easter Sunday. That's the "Good News"! April showers brings May flowers and June's moon,—then it's just a slip away into white linen summertime.

Ancient Chinese Spring Custom:

Three hundred and sixty eggs are stood up on end during the Vernal Equinox; if they stand without falling, it means good luck all year—and you will be in tune with the force of the universe. Winter's "yoke" lifts the day the eggs don't roll. When the sun pops in the sky, hope springs eternal. How can you not get excited by all that good luck coming to you? By the way, how do you like your eggs, up-or, over, opps . . . easy?

In conclusion, as the keeper of dreams spins yours on and around, may we all become custodians of the good life until next fall, while being better stewards of all the riches mother nature provides. Meanwhile, it's spring . . . and once again the voice of the turtle is heard in the land of New Fairfield, with no more teeth-chattering days left in the year we couldn't find winter!

Alfred Colo
1995

April Snow

When at last I'd hoped:
'The winter that wouldn't quit', would,
Another primer of snow,
Laced an unreceptive landscape,
With over coats or, thirsting,
Emerging buds, bursting—
With hope's spread wings of expectation,
For a sweeter, gentler, greener,
Change of scene.
Resigned tho' I,
To this 'element' of surprise,
Must be,
With delay's impatience,
To find reward,
Aft' a full melt and final thaw,
Welcomes spring once more,
To my front door;
Feast these two, too tired,
Cold, grey winter eyes,
With cascading arcs, not indoor,
Forced forsythia cuts,
But with hills of thrilling,
Spilling, mellow yellow daffodil.
April snow, go away.
Come again another way!
Who ever heard of shoveling rain?

Alfred Colo—2003

A Lion's Share Of April Snow

Just as we were all lulled into thinking that Spring was finally here, a done-deal, with sixty plus degrees on 1997's shiny Easter Sunday, a Nor' Easter deluged the Tri-State area with more snow than it could handle, or had seen all winter combined. A lion's share of heavy wet snow roaring out of March's last blast, gusting feet of white coverings on evergreens and not-yet-greens, leaving fallen trees, traffic snarls, and downed power lines in the wake of high winds, is no harbinger of spring to me, poetry about the subject notwithstanding.

Even as early heralds of crocus and daffodil, may have deluded us into thinking that spring had at last arrived, and we could safely store winter tools into Spring's tool shed, winter dropped its calling card; out again came shovels, snow blowers and sand for a hopefully-cautious last clean up.

We can't fool Mother Nature, though she sure can and did give us an April Fool's Day to long remember. Who'd-a-thunk that Spring could make such a complete about-face, deceive us into dropping our guard long enough to deliver winter's last knock-out punch? Unprepared? You bet!—Surprised? For sure!

Weren't we all still on a 'high' over Hale-Bopp's comet and its no-threat-trail of cosmic dust—to be slightly suspicious of an in-range local ominous sky? April snow reckoned to be rain, though not in this case.

Dare we suppose that all the convergings of Easter, Nor' Easter, comets and mass-cult-suicides, and talk of space ships, are signs of The Second Coming? No one knows for sure, nor can anyone accurately predict when that will occur. Meanwhile, just to be safe, button up your over coat; it ain't over till it's over!

Alfred Colo

Spring's Bouquet

Hedges of forsythia
Arc in yellow cascades,
Edging grass-green welcome mats,
Studded with golden dandelions.

Daffodils poke
Through leafy mulch,
Burst their bulbs
Into buttercups.

Croci, hyacinths, irises
And a band of bird calls
Tweet harmonics
Under nature's baton.

Lent, lily-white
With mourning,
Rises up each dawning,
With a blare of trumpets
From its heart,
Sounding Allelu-ias!

Alfred Colo—2005

Breath Of Spring

Never fear, welcome as cheer,
Spring's about to re-appear,
Warming frigid air,
With lilacs in her hair.
Robbins everywhere,
From all points south and west,
Have returned to nest,
Home—they love the best.

A breath of Spring
Is just the thing,
Our lungs swell up to see:
A whippoorwill chase up a hill,
Into a clump of trees,
Catch a balmy breeze,
Sing with ease, a trill;
Its throat about to spill.

Who doesn't need a fresh
Breath of Spring, so rare,
After winter's strangle-hold,
Gripped us numb, in cold despair?
Spring, about to hit its stride,
Invites the groom to wed his bride;
Kiss into bloom,—
The garden room outside.

Alfred Colo—2007

A Spring Thing

Out of a winter of darkness,
comes light with a brightness of spring,
tilting its veil,
'turning coat' and its tail
t'wards a stirring about ev'rything!

Out of the drear and the bleakness,
shines sun's warming rays all about,
budding hope in cold hearts,
lifting spirits with starts—
approaching the level of shout!

This SPRING THING is felt and designed to
create living's loveliest noise,
poised with music each year
titillating the ear,
inclined to awaken its joys!

Alfred Colo

Spring's Grand Awakening

It's been a long, long,
Snow-on-snow winter!
While anxiously awaiting
The drama to go,
I will not pretend,
I couldn't be happier, my friend,
To greet the green of grass,
And to bid farewell, alas,
To the cold and mass,
The slush and melt of snow.
In reality's land,
Where anything's probable,
Lady Spring welcomes
A new season in,
And the world is happily reborn.
In the land of fairy tales,
Where anything's possible,
Gnomes do likewise tell:
Of Spring's Grand Awakening.
So then, as it becomes important
To keep in tune and stay in touch
With nature's great out doors,
It becomes equally necessary
To slow down, and to refocus on:
The short-lived life of a crocus,
In a world, spinning too busily-
Even to notice:
They had come and gone!

Alfred Colo

Dawning

Grateful for a brand new blackboard,
upon which to chalk my day;
there to scratch imaginations,
must erase my cares away.
Thankful for a stretch of canvas,
thirsting for a painted sky,
budding branches fairly bursting,
color tints to rest an eye.

Now to layer-in a landscape
near a brook that gurgles by.
Add to this, in raucous tandem,
geese a gagg'ling as they fly.
Open up to me, Spring morning.
Fill my ears afresh with sound.
Brake the silences of Winter;
with a joyful noise, surround.

O creation, so long dormant,
now alive with sweet incense,
floating upward to its maker,
for the grace of His intents.

Dandelions, poking yellow,
heads above a sea of grass,
stir this lazy-lying fellow,
not to let the moment pass,
without noticing the shimmer,
in the rush and blush of Spring,
without savoring a soupcon
of the flavor life can bring!

Alfred Colo—1988

Old Sassafras

OLD SASSAFRAS,
  your undulating rusty trunk
    must have a treasure trove of flavorful tales
  behind that crusty bark.
And in the secret chambers of your sunken roots,
  as you twist around the balcony-
    to hug my home with sheltering.
A squirrel suddenly appeared, as if from nowhere,
  following the bend of a branch;
    first up, then down, then away in a lightening flash,
  swift as the lead car of a roller coaster,
    snapping its supple tail . . . . phfst!
New shoots appeared around the scar of a large limb
  under an overhang of roof;
Felled last fall, it stretched over a telephone line,
  in a futile attempt to call for help!
Elsewhere, other limbs hovered perilously close
  to the power line, whose 'hots' and 'colds'-
  spilled juice into the house, crying havoc,
    when it rubbed its nose too long against
  an old grown apple tree, the lone survivor
    of a long-gone orchard.
Blocked from a clear morning rising sun,
  I perused the newspaper, sipping O.J.,
    in an intrusive, unwelcome shade.
It was then that minor surgery came to mind.
Ironically, though notwithstanding,
  the dried root bark of this tree species is used in medicine.
Put to the test, the sharp teeth of my trusty pole saw,
  rasped and knashed until the leafy crest went . . . crash,
    falling helpless to the ground below the balcony,
  beside the garage door.

Regrettably, this branch of the tree's history
    was gone in an instant, cut off,—no more.
Swiftly then, the sun shone through, unfiltered,
    brightening thirsty, dark, untended house side shakes,
        which hadn't had a power wash, much less a stain,
    in many a season. I sat there, happily basking in its
face-warming rays upon my half-awake, and still lazy bones.

Unlike other trees, the sassafras has uncommon qualities, peculiar to itself; almost oriental, it is enduring, friendly, inviting and protecting. In its younger years there were no new-fangled TV antennas, to which its height might aspire. It had withstood the test of time and clime, of owl hoots, caws of crows, of nests and swings and other things. It just outgrew its owner's view of sun and pond. Sadly, it had to be trimmed to cater to the whim of its latest occupant of the Bavarian-Swiss style house, the late 'Jack Linner' built upon the stone foundation of old Satterlee's cowbarn. "Form follows function", came to mind to ease my conscience. When I later bent my back, to compactly dispose the remains of this latest prunning impulse. Farewell, OLD SASSAFRAS. Part of you goes with me, wherever, whatever verdure awaits your hereafter. When it comes my time to leave this place, I'd like to think I'll be up there too, for a bird's-eye-view of the ongoing history of steadfast, OLD SASSAFRAS. Finally, when you're ready to pack your torn and tattered trunk, I'll be looking back for you to lovingly sink your roots around my hereafter home.

Let your reassuring arms embrace our eternities, old friend. Be my tree-of-life once more, OLD SASSAFRAS of yore!

Alfred Colo—1986

Table of Contents Inside Looking Out

PART 3: SUMMER

Daylight Saving Sunset

Sun descends on a
daylight sunset sky,
one hour ahead of the spot,
it usually reserves for itself.

Up Coming Seasons

Prepare now for the
on-coming seasons,
while thinking of good reasons,
things grow green and lush,
and Spring is in the air.
Take advantage of
all your treasure there,
with full and loving
tenderness and watchful
patient care.

Alfred Colo—2005

More

Birds are more
than feathers and wings,
swallows and springs,
chirping at things;
Very much more than:
nesting their young,
breasting their bright,
colorful vesting among—
branches they perch on
with claws to have clung.

Birds at their best,
are warblers of song,
softening the air,
where they belong,
sharing their twitters,
sparkling and sweet,
zestful or honking
in a V-shap-ed fleet,
or popinjay-tweeting,
every-which-way,
all the day long.

If dogs're more than hair,
cats—more than fur-purring,
and shad, more than roe,
to keep 'em shad-roe-ing,
can we do any less
to keep on going?

Alfred Colo—1997

Birds And Blooms

Backyard-bird-buffs,
and flower fanciers,
use hundreds of tips
for bird attraction,
and growing gorgeous
garden action,
enjoying all the beauty
they create
in their
outdoor living rooms.

Alfred Colo—2005

Summer Rain

Summer Rain,
How welcome your pour;
The need of a struggling seed
Until now, you deem to ignore.
Summer Rain,
Your swellings are sweet
Relief from the sweltering
Heat off the brow.

Verdure and flowers
Shoulder the showers,
Which patter their faces;
Planted the while,
On each is a smile
Towards heavenly places.

Summer Rain,
Farmers and gardeners adore you,
For easing their efforts to grow,
For softening sods
With graces from God's
Assurance His blessings will flow.

Summer Rain,
Now silent the still of your voice,
Till gathering crowds
Of cumulus clouds
Recoup in a drill of their choice,
To quench every thirst once again,
And rejoice!

Alfred Colo—1997

Grass-Crabbing

Grass always looks greener
on the other side
of a fence,
except that this year,
it's browner here—
on every side.

Why must weather be
so extreme?
Some are scorched by it,
torched by it;
others are deluged in it,
grass is browned by it,
while others are drowned in it:
Everything's leveled
when the levees give,
so many die, and too few live.
Why can't weather
be more on the level?
Unfortunately,
we never get to choose,
who will win,-
who will lose.

My poor lawn's not asking
for a hurricane to water it,
just enough to keep it green,
tho' not too much
to slaughter it!
Water seeks its own level
in a spill-off.
Drought is the absence of rain,
and the color brown isn't green.

Why, in this, the best of
all possible worlds,
won't things get better,
if not wetter?
Must life always be seen as,
such a crap shoot?
All it would take
is a second weekend of
pouring rain,
to change my brown-dried lawn,
to a crisp grass-green again . . . .
so's I wouldn't need to
Crab about the grass anymore.

Alfred Colo—2005

We're Havin' A Heat Wave

The heat continues to make 'bad news' in the baking North East U.S., ever changing our shifting life styles. Hot air, not the slang version for empty or pretentious talk or writing, but the variety, characterized by a temperature higher than that of the human body and relatively abnormal high temperatures, very warm, as opposed to cold, is the thrust of this commentary about 'hot, dog days'—not the wiener kind . . . The oven got Fourth-of-July hot a week later than usual, sparing us the 3H: Hazy, hot and humid weather until now . . . Wow! It's a sizzler! Whoever said, "'t-ain't the heat, it's the HUM-I-DI-TY," got that right. The good news is that it's not a permanent heat wave, New Fairfielders.

It's going away . . . I promise you that . . . Trust me. Just imagine, it's only 190 some odd days until Christmas, so keep your shirts off, lest you get ruffled under the proverbial collar. "Don't put your spoon into a pot which does not boil for you," is a Romanian proverb, and Romanians know full well that there's nothing boiling here right now during these first dog days of summer, except the thermometer . . . Ouch!

The ancient Romans noted that the brightest star in the night sky—Sirius—kept appearing annually at the onset of hot, sultry weather. Somehow Serius—which stems from the Greek word for "scorcher"—became known as Dog Star, and the weather it heralded was named "dog days". Seriously, citizens, there's a whole kennel full coming in August, waiting to put the bite on us once again as well.

Science explains "dog days" thusly: Every July 3rd, the earth's northern hemisphere reaches its farthest point from the sun, approximately 94,510,000 miles. That point—the aphelion—ironically begins the hottest and stickiest days of the year. Temps that have been rising since spring will continue their upward climb until mid-July . . . And during every day of July, the chance of a thunderstorm will be 30 percent. Because the sun appears to stand still for a period of time, the length of day is approximately the same for about 10 days around the solstice. After June 25th, day length decreases by about one minute every three days until mid-July, when the diminishment speeds up to about two minutes a day. That, with no uncertain precision, spells the inevitable: summer winding down to its end . . . "Summertime and the livin' is easy. Fish are jumpin' and the cotton is high," but the heat leaves me totally 'cold,' no way in the cooling sense, nor dry . . . Talk about your perspiration . . . Whew! Quoting Robert Frost, "What happiness lacks in length, it makes up for in height," we may concur that summer is nice while it lasts, and the sun is pretty high too.

Summertime is great for beaches, which are safe when it's "TOO DARN HOT" for sharks to surface; in our inland waterways, we've nothing to fear. Report has it, moreover, that we eat more of them than they eat of us . . . So, go on, carnivores, have a bite. It's good for your J A W S!

So that grass won't brown and burn, take heed not to cut below 2 inches while the heat is on. Other precautions to take during this mid-summer sweat are: Drink at least 8 glasses of water a day, while avoiding alcohol and caffeinated drinks . . . Try to keep cool: use fans or air conditioning; follow the dog to the basement where it's cooler . . . Wear cool clothes: choose comfortable, light-weight, loose-fitting, light-colored clothing. Avoid the hotter polyesters and other synthetic materials.

A cool bath or shower removes excess heat 25 times faster than cool air. In a hurry? Run cool water over your wrists or place a cool wash cloth over your forehead or on the back of your neck. Avoid extra salt. Do not take salt tablets without a doctor's permission. On medication? Check with your doctor, pharmacist, or visiting nurse or home health aide for advice on how to best protect yourself against heat-related illness. Medications such as those for high blood pressure and depression—reduce your ability to fight heat effectively during a heat wave . . . Never ignore the body's physical or mental warning signals, when it's struggling with heat. If mild signals such as feeling hot and bothered, feeling tired, or loss of appetite persist, seek medical advice.

Alfred Colo

Now You See It . . . Now You Don't

Since 1998, when a backyard pine tree had been felled due to a blight, its two feet tall stump remained to form a practical pedestal for my classic grey garden urn, I decorated with a different annual variety each year since the demise, to lend a touch of color to an otherwise 'ho-hum' view from the north side of home. This year, however, I noticed a rise and fall in its growth, which never seemed to mound properly, or crest in bloom to my satisfaction; suspecting foul play, I arose earlier than usual one morning, to catch a doe breakfast—ing on my wanna-be visual work of art. Beside this feng shui arrangement, a vibrant-colored orange lily surprised me with its presence, as if to atone for the doom of the urn-filled arrangement, which literally did not get off the ground enough to satisfy my initial visual intention, NOR to console me in my grief.

Dismayed, I decided then, to remove the urn from harm's way, closer to the house, and noticed that the stump, after almost a decade of exposure, had begun to disintegrate; its bark peeled off quite readily to the slightest pull. So, with more determination than grit, I planned on removing it; easier said than done: Too-hot sunshine, followed by ensuing rain in the days ahead, stalled my aim, just enough to allow my aching muscles to restore their over-stretched sinues. I did manage, before I called it quits, to chop up two pails full of the riches, metaphorically filling up the urn with its remains, ready to spread. The center of the stump remained too firm to whittle away this day, doubtless requiring several more years of exposure and rot, before the rest of it is loose enough to remove.

Preparing to tackle the job of removal, I sought and retrieved every imaginable pick, axe, saw and garden tool I thought necessary for helping to spare my digits, but resorted to no more than one or two tools to finish, without running off to the shed each time I needed the proper tool. I hesitated to take a chain saw to it, fearing a gearing entanglement if I got too close to the dirt level; being reluctant to repeat another clogging I last year took to Peerless to clean and restore. Hiring a stump grinder would be quicker, though more costly, so I weighed my options, deciding to do it the hard way.

Finally, I found a way to recycle this garden gold, by mulching nearby tree bases; (stumps to stumps,) so to speak. Guess the bewildered deer must need to sup in a new stomp, than from the delicacies of my disappearing stump. Looking for advice, I approached Helen, my knowledgeable garden neighbor, how she managed to protect her yucca plants' white flower clusters from being chewed down as mine frustratingly were.

"I use an automatic sprinkler system to spook them," adding, "If ya don't stay a step ahead of the little darlings, they'll eat you out of house and garden, as do the ground hogs abounding here with their equally hardy appetites."

Sadly, they'll never see beauty's creativity through my eyes of appreciation, but rather, as a substance to line their fat bellies, each free-lunch they can get.

Were I dumb as they, could I be faulted for striving to survive, this far afield from their own natural habitats?

Were I smart as they, would I allow a little stump to trip up my way? . . . I'd just search for another pit stop, to irk another gardener.
The 'buck' doesn't only stop here!

Alfred Colo—July 2007

Among The Branches

For most kids, there's nothing
quite like climbing a tree—
the thrill of discovery,
finding that perfect perch,
from which to survey the world,
or disappear into the secret reaches
of a leafy canopy.
AMONG THE BRANCHES.
To create a tree house,
think like a child;
to dwell among the branches,
be a child.
A tree house must never overpower
the tree in which it is built;
and it should sit snugly,
if not lightly—in its sheltering arms . . .

Protected from weather and adults,
tho' it be an earthly dwelling,

the house can evoke
a whimsically lobsided air,
with a rough-hewned ladder,
or a hand-carved stair,
an appropriate sign or two, like:
Duck—at each landing entrance.

Beneath an asymmetrical, shingled roof,
can be a cozy reading and game corner;
outside, a pulley-attached-basket
for delivery of snacks and toys.
Such a kid-scaled, cozy hut, can
fast become a favorite,
enchanted hide-a-way,
through growing years of playful—

exploration outside, above ground,
reaching for dreams,
high as the sky, free as a bird—
AMONG THE BRANCHES, testing the wind.

Alfred Colo—August 2007

All Day Long

All day long,
under flesh-scorching sun,
I'll paint on the run,
with raptures of fun,
the poetry of music,
sweet scents of flowers,
still lifes and scenes,
unmindful of hours,
tick-timing
seconds and minutes
of this summer season away.
All day long,
with word hues at hand,
on canvas command,
I'll capture a place,
detail a face,
wide-eyed with
green pools of grace,
gazing out,

still-posed in space,
watching the sea swells
take turns to race
their white caps to shore,
crashing in splashes
on air strips of sand,
sea gulls adore
not to ignore,
and, where sand pipers band
all day long
getting tanned.
There's where I pitch my
tent and stand,
to word-wash with salt spray,
all I survey,
all day long,
and it's grand!

Alfred Colo

Summer Gathering

What a welcoming sight
is a potpourri of beautiful
backyard songbirds:
from a dazzling red cardinal,
to the vibrant bluebird and goldfinch,
to an orange-bellied robin,
gathered for a
birdbath refreshment bash.

Such an impromptu "gathering" is—
one of summer's cherished sights:
striking, stunning, and incredibly real,
in a breathless array of living colors,
meticulously wrought by
a caring Creator's higher power,
to entertain, as they too,
are entertained in summer assembly,
to which all other creatures
are invited to marvel
at this truly remarkable,
captivating gift of nature,
captured in close harmony.
Unity such as this,
though not often planned,
and seldom by design,
is meant for us all to take note,
as we ourselves, gather in Summer,
unfettered and featherless!

Alfred Colo—2005

Winged Wonders

Bring on the wings, a bounty of things
To attract the hummers with sure-fire things.
Roll out the red carpets for hummingbirds and butterflies!
Bring them flocking; keep them happy,
While you enjoy their show!
Make your own garden a "hot spot" for hummers—
On sunny, torrid, midsummer days.
Liven up your pied-a-tere with nature's winged jewels.
Flock the flutterers to their favorite garden, yours—
With love, humor, and observation and color.
Attract a treasure trove of winged wonders
To feed, water and shelter, and play.
Be fascinated by their behavior,
From dances to duels, bright with butterflies
And buzzing with hummers in "prime time" season.
From nesting to nurturing,
Mating to wooing, fill your garden retreat.
Allow God's wonders to tickle your funny bone,
And to lift your spirits a beat, in the heat.
Feel the love connection
As they feed from your finger, and
While winged wonders yet linger . . . SMILE!

Alfred Colo

August . . . .

the month of
rosy Sharon bloom,
gets too uncozy
to garden-groom
nature's outdoor living room.
When August grass
burns brown a lot,
'cause clouds pass by,
not on this spot;
and rain barrels
run on empty
in upper nineties swelter,
search for shelter!
Perhaps, before this summer ends,
and fall prepares to follow,
August intends for us to wallow
under a willow a while—
with a smile, or—
stretched out like a ground hog laid,
on a flat bed rock out in the shade, or—
follow your dog
below basement grade,
laid-back 'till
August dog-days fade,
sipping a swallow of
iced-glass cool,cool
lemonade!
Beer drinkers too,
can have it made!

Alfred Colo—2005

Take Time To Smell The Flowers

TAKE TIME TO SMELL THE FLOWERS
To break away, a while;
To make up for the hours
When you can't or, won't smile.
Take time to soak in sunshine;
It can be so much fun,
Relaxing—when taxing—and boring things
Are done away with—and done!
It's time to tell the 'powers'
That send us up a wall:
There's no need more important
Than to heed nature's call.
Take time to put your noses
Where roses ramble free.
Make time to meander when blossoms bloom
And share their perfume with me.
TAKE TIME TO SMELL THE FLOWERS
While you're still in the pink.
How many mortal hours
Do we have, do you think?
So when your world goes 'crazy',
Get lazy for a spell,
And you will look fresh
As a daisy does,
Because you took time to
Smell, not to stomp through
The flowers!

Alfred Colo

Summer Swan Song

Hold on to summer
Until it's really gone, o'er,
Time for a change.
Yea, summer can be more
If we hold its essence hostage
A little while longer:
List'ning for the ocean in its shells,
Beholding the fluttering motion of its
butterflies,
Savoring nature's sweetness in its berries,
And capturing the pungent flavors in its
spices,
Plucking the rip'ning riches of its produce
And wafting, waning perfume from its
flow'rs.
Until time runs out,
Don't be quick to bid "goodbye" to
summer,
Nor to shout "hello" to fall just yet.
You'll know it's time for a change
When autumn puts a spin
On leaves skipping loose,
From trees stripping thin;
Cool winds working in.
'Til the wake-up-call
On a different season
Is heard by all,
Hark, in a word—
To summer's swan song bird!

Alfred Colo

Reluctant

I don't long to say 'farewell' to Summer,
Not until the swans have sung their song,
I must cling a wee bit more to Summer,
Watching geese formations wing along,
Everything in due time has a season;
Summer time was come and's almost gone.
Now's the time for fall to sneak a breeze in—
Through the closing door it knocks upon.
I can't greet 'hello' in truth to Autumn,
Not now for a little longer while,
Not until the summer I'll remember,
Bids September walk an Autumn mile.

Uninclined to pack the things of Summer,
I've a mind to stack the wears I must.
Summer's fading fast in 'fallen leavings',
Trailing in the blast of autumn's dust.
Every time and clime, to some are pleasin';
Summer trees in season gowns must go.
'Tis the time for fall to try to squeeze in
Through the door, ajar, its fashion show.
I'm not ready now to welcome Autumn,
Which seems heady now to strut its style . . .
So, I'll tarry on a trifle longer,
At the turn of summer's gate a while,
Til the blush of Autumn makes me smile!

Alfred Colo

Table of Contents Inside Looking Out

PART 4: FALL

Season Change

Ready to fall,
autumn leaves burn
in uneasy crowns,
their bridges of
no return;
dead on arrival,
in lusterless,
uneven clusters—
of browns.

Sensing a turn
on the subtle curve
of transition's wheel,
intent upon autumn's heel,
summer waves goodbye
and welcome to—
a new season change.

Bounties are bursting,
plenteous o'er,
dressed in immense
blessings, it wore;
burgeon in stockings
of harvest's outpour,
stored in the tallest
silo on site,
beside the door of
autumn's welcome to winter,
and snow, white-bright.

Alfred Colo—2007

Fall Designs

Days get shorter.
Nights last longer.
There's a nip in the air.
s' Time to pull on
A long-sleeved wool-on-
'n' Set in a rocking chair,
By the fire,
nice 'n' cozy,
Sippin' hot cocoa brown.
Gazin' at embers,
As October's
Days are dwindlin' down.
While we're heading
For flannel bedding,
Comfy, welcome and warm,
Trees are wearing,
Gowns, so daring,
No 'Versace' could form!

Alfred Colo, 9/97

Where There Is No Autumn

I wanna go south,
Where there is no autumn,
Breaking into colours,
Where the cold doesn't crouch
Like a sleeping lion,
Waiting to pounce.

Then again,
A horrid hurricane season,
Can give my mind good reason,
To invest in a new snow blower,
And endure another,
Harsh cold winter, more secure.
Retirement in the South
Can be a disappointment cruel,
When you're under water, not for pleasure.
Weighing both: which is worse?
When's the cure a curse?
Summer won't last forever;
Shorter days and longer nights
Are coming.
Which way are you going?
I know I'll be missing
The absent summer
We never had
And try hard
Not to be sad.
This snow bird's
Flying back home, north east,
Where the greater of two evils is least.

Alfred Colo—2004

The Ninth Month

The ninth month—in September,
Migrants start to fly,
August passes by, and—
Bird-watched-summers die.

An apple-butter-sky,
Returns in Autumn then,
Without a falling leaf, a thorn,
An ear of corn to wonder:

Why October, cider-sober,
Every year,
Turns ten to cheer,
Being born again!

Alfred Colo—2006

Sneak Peek

This year's autumn foliage,
commenced an early peak;
its hues are turning faster
by the minute, week to week.

Leaf-peepers, wont to watch the best,
fall splendors start to plum,
from yellow ash, dash forth to see
some orange maples. Come.

Move quickly. Catch an early blast:
leaf-luster is good reason;
trust cluster, destined not to last
beyond the harvest season.

Out then, sneak a peek at:
purple sumac and bronzed beech,
sparkling jewels in nature's crown,
dried out in easy reach,

spread in caches of rusted curls,
in carpets on the ground,
for adults and their kin to kick in,
all the fun they found.

Alfred Colo—2005

Just A Scream Away . . . .

Halloween is just a scream away.
Look for special goose bumps as you play;
That'll quicken your breath,
And nearly scare you to death!
AT 'trick-or-treat' time,
Ring-a-chime-time's neat,
When a treat is a sweet,
And scares,—just a scream away.
On 'All-Hallows, goblins'll get-cha,
If nothin's-a-gobbled you yet.
Black cats and witches
Won't keep you in stitches,
So come well-prepared, my pet!
Don't dress 'to the nines'—
For the prowl of your life,
On the night you must work up a lather.
By the light of the moon,
Croon that 'horror-night' tune:
"A Ghost Of A Chance", as ye gather.
When lit pumpkins grin ear-to-eery,
With smiles that would make dentists leery,

Tho' harmlessly ruthless,
You'll laugh yourselves toothless,
With shrieks, rather useless, my dearie.
Knowing that you saved your neck too,
By the skin of your teeth,
You won't know you're dead,
Or cling by a thread.
Oops! Sorry, if I spoke too soon.
Did I lose your head? Well . . . . ,
Ya shoulda stood in bed!
It'll be one wicked night in October,
So, don't think you'll drink yourself sober;
Yet bats if you do, drive, even if you—
Are native to Manitoba.
Wooo, Ha! Ha! . . . Wheee! Mamma!
Can you wait? Don't miss it! Catch it!
Halloween's—like, just a scream away . . . !
Stay street-smart; devilish creatures are out.
Unless you know what's about,
You'll never got out—of this world-alive!
Boo! Gotcha!

Alfred Colo

No Boundaries

A tree knows no boundaries, but
Spills its leaves on two sides,
Regardless of where its trunk is rooted.
When uprooted, it shares its broken self
With neighbors, part and parcel.
The true test of good neighborliness is—
Who gets to clean it up.
Be wise, discuss the burden's best solution.
A tree knows no boundaries,
Sharing its shade, each side alike.
So, why cry over broken branches?
If tempted to grumble
When leaves on you tumble,
Remember to humble yourself.
Don't leaf-blow leaves
From whence they came.
Why look for someone to blame?
Make leaves a sharing—game:
Grin and bear it.
Cart and care it—
Mulches fine, good as gold—
On either side of property's line . . . .

Alfred Colo

Fancy Fall

Snap the splendors of Autumn.
Track the foliage of Fall.
Step out. Look about, ye peepers of leaves;
Take in the beauty of it all!
Admire the first colors
On drives in the country,
In hiking and on biking routes,
And links to state forests and parks.
Explore less-trodden paths,
Off the more beaten track;
Some of the choice views
Are closer than the pack on your back.
Where the sun is warm,
And the sky is blue,
And the folk in good spirits
Are welcoming too,
Is the place for you.
Take in a local fest, and
Run into old friends,
You've not seen in a while.
Pick some apples at an orchard.
Let a plump, ripe pumpkin,
Cut out for laughs, make you smile.
Oh, and don't forget the colors
That peak in the middle of the month,
View this year's promised, rich display,
There for young and old to behold, on a day,
Just a windfall away this Fall, and
Last, but not least,
Bring a bit of Autumn to a bedside,
When you pay the ill a call . . . .
And you will more than ever,
FANCY FALL'S reward!

Alfred Colo—2004

The Hills Are Alive

The hills are alive
With bright hues of Autumn,
On palettes of green,
Russet, orange and gold.

The hills are alive,
Picture-perfect viewing,
In another week
They will 'peak', I'm told.

If you haven't yet,
Feast your eyes on the scene,
That occurs every Fall.
You'll not soon forget,
The sheer majesty
Of it all!

The hills are alive,
Dressed for chill October;
Leaves luster like jewels
In a breezy crown.

When hills look alive
In their royal-robed splendor,
You'll know
The best show
Did arrive in town.

Alfred Colo—1993

October Flies

October flies arise indoors;
Inside the window storms.
Some are caught behind the screens,
unyet removed, to dorm.
There they wallow in the warmth,
Out of harm's way . . . until
I espyed their nesting place;
Intruders, rue the day.
Farewell, October flies, goodbye!
The season's over now.
I've had my fill of screening you out,
and will not screen you in!
Prepare to move. Shoo, fly! Oh, my!
My temper's rising, hot.
Beware. Be wise or die today—
One at a time from sssss . . . . wat!
Time flies, but not when you're counting.
October flies,
Same time next year?
Only if you're a lucky one,
Who didn't get to stay,
And got away from here.

Alfred Colo

Jewels Of Midnight

The allure and romance of night
is captured in stunning re-creation
of bright and pure enchantment
under midnight's spell.

Shimmering against an exquisite sky,
cushioned in mysterious velvet,
a spectacular necklace
of crystalline stars,
strung in opulent radiance,
shapes a luminous and breathtaking
panorama of classic beauty.
Cherished through ages past,
it shall be worn to last,
by new generations of
avid sky watchers,
captivated by midnight's spell,
enclosed in heaven's jewel box.

Alfred Colo—2005

Exit

Autumn leaves are falling fast,
In a sudden weather cast's
Prediction of a frosty blast,
Prior to harvest.

Limpid leaves are curling up,
Stirring up, swirling up,
Showing up in reds and amber brown
In crazy-quilted beds of comfort—down.

Differing from snow, fallen leaves
Never melt, tho'are heard,
Crunching-up, bunching-up,
In each cozy niche, winds direct they go.

Autumn leaves are falling fast,
Summer's past, Fall's arrived,
Soon we're left to wonder,
Comes a driven snow,

Where did they all go?
Had a one survived?

Alfred Colo—2006

Last Chance

The last leaf of a dying tree
shivers on a limb, helplessly,
unwilling to let go,
afraid to face the wind alone.

Nothing left to cling to,
last chance to show its colors,
one chance left to live
before it snows,
to fly, to fall,
to dance, to die.

Alfred Colo—2005

Autumn Bliss

Hazy autumn sunlight
Filtered through the trees;
The air was frought with fragrance,
And apple-crisp with breeze.

Crank the choppers.
Feed the hoppers.
Watch the amber flow.
Only a few left to go—
Mellow afternoons
Would grace the fall
Before snow storms
Sweep across and put
The fall to sleep.

After fresh cider's bouquet
Is sipped and stored for winter,
Potluck parties, lengthening shadows,
And honks of geese, heading north,
Hinted that; chore-time was near.

Each cider sip
Would not only taste of
Fall's bounteous jug,
But also joys shared
On one golden afternoon's
Country hug, and tender kiss,
Is Autumn bliss.

Alfred Colo—2006

Scarecrow

Pumpkin and corn stalks,
Tatters 'n tails . . .
Top-hatted scarecrow's
The style that prevails.
Form'lly attired
'Cept for dungarees,
He's scaring nobody,
And knocks his own knees . . .
Out in a field,
Propped up to stand guard,
He'll chase off intruders,
Though not very hard.
In a breeze flaps he—
At man, beast or bird,
Scarecrow is scary
With narry a word.
He tilts like a vane
When weather winds blow,
But rather were wed,
'Stead-a scarin' a crow!

Alfred Colo—1995

An Autumn Royal

Fulsome is the crown nature shares,
Ere it bares its bits;
Lovely are the jewels Autumn wears-
On the head it fits.
Precious do they gleam,
Shim'ring in her hair,
Whilst a breeze is up,
Seeming to cavort
In a jovial sport
'Round a regal cup.
Royal is the reign,
Tho' too brief the span
For rich robes to wear;
In the show-of-shows,
Ev'ry viewer near
Knows enough to care:
Splendor that is here,
Sun-dried for a spell,
Abdicates the chair,
now no longer there.
Save for shutter clicks,
Captured raptures' mix
Of unshy camera pix,
Autumn Royal, alas,
For one brief moment's pass,
Has come, as if,—to Camelot.

Alfred Colo—1997

O November

O NOVEMBER,
cold and damp and gray November,
will you act like this for long,
cheerless as a birdless song,
chilling as the churning air,
spilling, turning here and there,
willing to blow anywhere,
O NOVEMBER?
Wait 'n' see's my attitude,
and I'll greet with gratitude,
forecasts plainly visible,
'stead-a drear and 'drizzible'.

O NOVEMBER,
finally, when all comes down:
leaves, rain show'rs,
et al come down,
ere Thanksgiving turkeys,
and Kris Kringle come to town,
will your digits freeze my crown,
leaving me as 'down' as feathers,
this NOVEMBER?

Alfred Colo

Inside Looking Out

On a grey and wet post Thanksgiving day, the south side of the garden, put to sleep and now at rest, has nothing to cheer about except for the colors of Christmas: a circular green wired mulch bin with a red leaf mix, anchors the east end of the yard at the foot of a forty something old, pink dogwood, sporting its seasonal red berries, over the mulch pile, looking like a Christmas wreath. On the south east side center, pachysandra ground cover surrounds the base of a Japanese red maple tree, planted in 1968 as a memorial, stretching its naked branches skyward, like intertwined octupi, still bearing its wounds from a recent trimming by the new re-roofer, as a precaution against wind damage to its brittle edges.

The late-cut, over grown lawn resulting from this November's unseasonably mild weather, is still strewn with late falling leaves, compacting on the fast hardening ground, enclosed in a green metal fence, lined with red barberry bushes, camouflaging a neighbor's ratty-looking left overs from his raised ground and bucket vegetable garden.

The east end had earlier been planted with a trio of shoots from a multi colored rose of sharon bush, to resolve my feng shui attempt at block out of this eye sore. A 40's TV ariel was dismantled from its old perch for the new roof's ridge vent and to update my overall reception with cable vision, after a disheartening five time attempt at installation.

It'll take better weather days to get me to rake up the last autumn leaves, some still waving farewell to Fall before they eventually do . . . fall too.

The east side stone wall steps up to a higher level, holds my this year's sorely neglected non-attempt at vegetable gardening, nature clogged with weeds of its own, whose rotting wood fence, still supports an invasive trumpet vine, reserving its blare of announcements from its red instruments until Spring.

The rear house garden lawn, surrounded with trees and forsythia shrubs, yet unshed, reveals a new mulch pile on one end of a naturally formed garden sanctuary. A blue colored empty water drum, stands up-ended beside the garden shed, along side my trusty, rusty folding garden cart, still rolling, despite severe damage to its tubless tires, with Autumn things awaiting storage in the shed.

The immediate West side, rear house garden, anchored by a twin white birch tree, also planted in memorium, shows a central well cap, with an original, now decorative only, garden pump, spoking into irregular blue-stone paths, past the yuccas, planted over a septic tank. Left of this are my colorful harbingers-of-Christmas-collection of bowling balls, neatly spaced like bocci balls, ready to blow away the garden pickets, resembling rows of bowling pins in an alley.

Halloween has long since past, still baring bare-boned skeletons of trees, left to remind me of the shivers coming, not the kind which raise your head hair, but ones which cause your skin to bump.

Dips in the landscape beyond the property land marks, now reveal just the peaks of homes in neighborly distance behind a new fence leaf barrier I installed, low enough not to block the view, but aimed at catching moving leaves caught in a gust and blown my way for pickup. Four rakings and then some a season is just about enough to handle for this, still healthy 79er, a bit put upon by neighbors' neglected pickups, now inside looking out and forward to a new Advent/Christmas season, fast approaching.

The North side of this visual tour, front of the cottage garden, reveals some lingering vestiges of seasonal color: a blue gazing ball left on a terra cotta pedestal, stands beacon-like, centered amid a cluster of multi-colored mums, last year, pre-maturely nipped off at the bud by hungry, eager deer out for breakfast. It had been suggested by someone in-the-know, that I sprinkle moth crystals as a deterrent; further, just to play it safe, I caged in this area with an see-through enclosure, tall enough to thwart rubber-necking. The success of this ingenuity, extended the life and color of this enclave, visible from the kitchen, for appreciation, well beyond the fair-game deer eat-outs.

A box of frost-bitten, now waning pink petunias, drooped in melancholy, awaiting a mulch pile.

At the end of the North side's property line lawn, is a blank space, now missing a withered hydrangea bush, which hadn't survived the last Winter's onslaught, nor did an unprotected rhododendron, I replaced with some hardier and more colorful rose of sharon, beside a struggling Japanese red maple, I'll give until spring to respond, before it gets the axe too-of sayonara. Unless properly shielded from wind and frost, these expensive treasures cannot withstand winter's ravages. Trial and error can be costly and time consuming.

Branches from too-close house trees, trimmed by the roofer, lay at the ramp, stubbs out, in a pool of leaves, awaiting a long-over-due promised dumpster pickup.

The side of the house facing Ball Pond, saw some needed and expensive improvemnets: a newly installed wrought iron fence on a six feet high patio, fronting the main entrance, replaced a weathered, white-painted, fretted fence, whose attached pole lantern was replaced by an old wrought iron, restored light fixture, given by my brother, now ably lighting the approaching stone steps. I wreathed the base of this for holiday decor and secured a sculptured wire deer to the opposite end stone column, as if a reminder of such destructive pests was needed. Further, a new automatic motion-detector-light fixture was installed over the garage for visibility and deterence. The iron-monger replaced my old name sign with a proper, fancier one, extending from the stone column, left of the steps. This about wraps up another season-in-the-red, certain to reveal a new year of surprises from the Inside Looking Out, at black and white, towards the colors of spring.

Alfred Colo (year ending 2005)